WINGS OF FIRE

WINGS OF FIRE

POEMS BY CHARLES GHIGNA

ILLUSTRATIONS BY PATRICIA SEE HOOTEN

Druid Press
Birmingham, Alabama

Wings of Fire
By Charles Ghigna
Illustrations by Patricia See Hooten

ISBN Number: 0-945301-08-1

Copyright © Druid Press, 1992

Druid Press
2724 Shades Crest Road
Birmingham, Alabama 35216

ACKNOWLEDGMENTS

Seven of these poems first appeared with seven poems by X. J. Kennedy in *Sticks.* My thanks to editor Mary Veazey for her permission to reprint them here.

*for all saints
and sinners*

CONTENTS

But if the archangel now, perilous,
from behind the stars took even one
step down toward us: our own heart,
beating higher and higher, would
beat us to death. Who are you?

—Rainer Maria Rilke
Duino Elegies, 2

I

SOLACE

We follow
separate
sidewalks

to the
cathedral
steps.

We climb
together,
open the door

and enter
the sanctuary
of each other.

Parting Shadows

Your lips are the poem
I enter to write
myself back into being.

They open into that place
where two dark angels
sit in a screaming church.

They whisper the sweet sin
of flying the night
with nowhere to land.

Their winged words
lift us into each other
and tell us who we are.

WINGS OF FIRE

We rise and fall
touching, retouching
ourselves with each other.

We open and close
coming, coming back
to the burning light.

We dare this dance
as one with the
unforgiving flame.

This is our fire.
We are the wings
of its moth.

II

SECOND EVE

When you pass by
the weeping willow stops,
stands tall,

becomes the apple tree
whose fruit is sweeter
than God.

CONFESSION

I am no angel.
I have tasted
the wine of your lips.

Now I cannot quench
this burning need
to fly.

VESPERS

Icons in the dark,
we press against
the ancient stone.

Your warm temples
listen to my litany
of whispered prayers,

to the rosary
I cannot
stop saying.

III

After Mass

We rise
in the unholy dark
and walk to the window.

We look out
for the future,
but find instead

only pieces of red,
a pattern of stains
on the broken glass.

Silent Vows

I kneel before
you, you kneel
before me.

We pray
at the altar
of our egos.

AT THE SIGN OF THE CROSS

We are the prey
of each other.
We pray for each other.

Our sin is the sin
of praying
with sin.

Our penance
is the act
of contradiction.

We are at the cross.
Let us not altar
our past.

IV

ACOLYTES

We carried
our torch
to the altar.

We touched
its flame
with our flame.

The fire
we shared
speaks in tongues,

an ardent choir
of votive
candles.

THE FATHER,
THE SON AND
YOUR HOLY GHOST

I kneel
to tuck my son
into his bed

and see again
your face
upon the night.

I bow my head
in prayer
for what I have,

for only what
my closing eyes
can hold.

EVENING REVERIE

Again
I close
my eyes

and enter
this dream
of you.

Even
in my dreams
I am dreaming.

V

Hallelujah

I turn on
the radio
and ride

the air
waves
to church.

The choir
on stage
is the same,

but my lips
sing a solo
of you.

SOTTO VOCE

Though your
words were
rare,

your lips
told me
more

in their
delicious
silence

than all
the words
that I

have
never
said.

ACT OF CONTRITION

You needed more
than prayers
to put the light

back in your
dark eyes.
There was no way

I could change things,
no way I could leave
without holding you.

We both saw it coming.
We both lost hold
of the light.

VI

EQUAL RITES

We close our eyes
to the distance
between us

and curse
our need
for communion.

We will not
rise
from our knees

and walk
down the aisle
to the altar.

We will not
swallow this
Eucharist of Silence.

Deliver Us Not

It is here
away
from the world

that I fly
back
to that place

where prayers
and you
come true.

I light
in the shadows
again,

on earth
as it is
in this haven.

Devotion

Our blind faith
in this litany
of unanswered prayers

continues to grow,
a catechism
of our confirmation,

a new testament
to our first
holy communion.

Patricia See Hooten is a graphic designer and illustrator working in Birmingham, Alabama.

Charles Ghigna is poet-in-residence at the Alabama School of Fine Arts in Birmingham.